D1116424

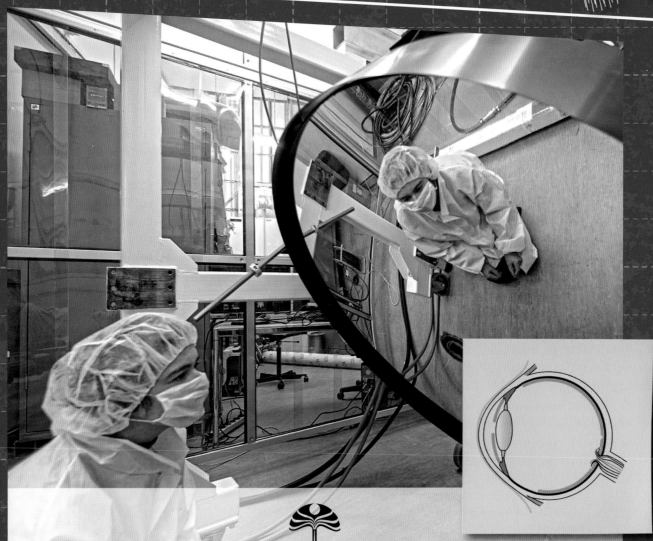

OPTICAL ENGINEERING
AND THE Science of Light

Crabtree Publishing Company
www.crabtreebooks.com

Anne Rooney

ENGINEERING IN ACTION

Crabtree Publishing Company
www.crabtreebooks.com

Author: Anne Rooney
Publishing plan research and development:
   Reagan Miller
Project coordinator: Kathy Middleton
Photo research: James Nixon
Editors: Paul Humphrey, James Nixon, Rachel Eagen
Proofreader: Wendy Scavuzzo
Layout: sprout.uk.com
Illustrations: sprout.uk.com
Cover design and logo: Margaret Amy Salter
Production coordinator and prepress
   technician: Tammy McGarr
Print coordinator: Margaret Amy Salter

Produced for Crabtree Publishing Company by
Discovery Books

Photographs:
Corbis: pp. 7 (Maximilian Stock Ltd/Science Faction),
   14 (Greg Dale/National Geographic Society), 15
   bottom (Jim Craigmyle), 21 (Roger Ressmeyer), 24
   (Peter Ginter/Science Faction).
NASA: pp. 5, 25 top (ESA/L. Calcada [ESO for STScI]),
   25 bottom (Dominic Hart).
Rex Images: p. 17 top (Moviestore Collection).
Science Photo Library: pp. 11 bottom (Patrice
   Latron/Look At Sciences), 22 (Hubert Raguet/
   Look At Sciences), 29 (Lawrence Berkeley National
   Laboratory).
Shutterstock: cover (except top left and right and
   bottom right), pp. 4 (chaoss), 8 (SSSCCC), 11 top
   (Vladimir Sazonov), 15 top (Sergey Galushko), 16
   top (Winai Tepsuttinun), 16 bottom
   (bikeriderlondon), 17 bottom (antb), 18 (Goodluz),
   19 bottom (Sergey Nivens), 20 (1000 Words), 23
   (Farferros), 26 (Andrea Danti), 28 (Pavel K).
Thinkstock: cover (top left and right and bottom right).
Wikimedia: pp. 9 bottom (ESO), 12 top and bottom, 13
   left (www.rijksmuseum.nl), 13 right (Dartmouth
   Electron Microscope Facility, Dartmouth College),
   19 top (Frank Schulenberg), 27 (Wikiphoto).

Library and Archives Canada Cataloguing in Publication

Rooney, Anne, author
      Optical engineering and the science of light / Anne Rooney.

(Engineering in action)
Includes index.
Issued in print and electronic formats.
ISBN 978-0-7787-1228-2 (bound).--ISBN 978-0-7787-1232-9
(pbk.).--ISBN 978-1-4271-8950-9 (pdf).--ISBN 978-1-4271-8946-2
(html)

      1. Optical engineering--Juvenile literature. 2. Optics--Juvenile
literature. I. Title. II. Series: Engineering in action (St. Catharines,
Ont.)

TA1521.R66 2013   j621.36   C2013-906147-9
                                        C2013-906148-7

Library of Congress Cataloging-in-Publication Data

Rooney, Anne.
   Optical engineering and the science of light / Anne Rooney.
      pages cm -- (Engineering in action)
   Audience: Ages 10-13.
   Audience: Grades 4 to 6.
   Includes index.
   ISBN 978-0-7787-1228-2 (reinforced library binding) -- ISBN
978-0-7787-1232-9 (pbk.) -- ISBN 978-1-4271-8950-9 (electronic pdf) --
ISBN 978-1-4271-8946-2 (electronic html)
   1. Optical engineering--Juvenile literature. 2. Light--Juvenile
literature. I. Title.

TA1521.R66 2014
621.36--dc23

                                        2013035441

Crabtree Publishing Company

Printed in Canada/102013/BF20130920

www.crabtreebooks.com   1-800-387-7650

Published in Canada
Crabtree Publishing
616 Welland Ave.
St. Catharines, ON
L2M 5V6

Published in the United States
Crabtree Publishing
PMB 59051
350 Fifth Avenue, 59th Floor
New York, New York 10118

Published in the United Kingdom
Crabtree Publishing
Maritime House
Basin Road North, Hove
BN41 1WR

Published in Australia
Crabtree Publishing
3 Charles Street
Coburg North
VIC, 3058

CONTENTS

WHAT IS OPTICAL ENGINEERING?

Optics is the science of light. Optical engineers work with many technologies to use and control light. Over the last five centuries, optical engineering has given us telescopes, glasses, photography, film, broadband networks, and TV. It is a world-changing area of work.

Putting light to work

Optical engineers work with vision and light. They design instruments we look through, such as cameras or microscopes. They also work with **telecommunications**, **optometry**, **solar power**, **lasers**, and animation.

THE DESIGN PROCESS

When an optical engineer takes on a new project, he or she follows an eight-step process to design, build, and test a solution (see diagram):

Every time you take a photo with a camera or your phone, you're relying on the work of optical engineers.

Steps in the design process:

Identify the problem

↓

Identify criteria and constraints

↓

Brainstorm possible solutions

↓

Select a design

↓

Build a model or prototype

→

Test the model and evaluate

Refine the design

↓

Share the solution

Moving light around: The most basic tools for controlling light are lenses and mirrors. These are key parts of even very complicated pieces of optical equipment. They are used to change the direction in which light travels, and to **focus** or scatter light. They are often components in extremely complex and delicate systems.

THE FIRST OPTICAL ENGINEERS?

It's said that the Greek mathematician and scientist Archimedes invented a "death ray" to destroy a fleet of Roman ships approaching the city of Syracuse around 213 BCE. He set up curved bronze mirrors to focus the rays of the Sun on the ships and set them on fire. Two hundred years earlier, the playwright Aristophanes had mentioned using a glass stone to melt wax by focusing the Sun's rays.

Light and sight

The science of optics relates to how and what we see, and it requires a good understanding of how the eye and brain work together. Some optical engineers work specifically in optometry—the medical science of correcting vision. The science of eyesight was a foundation for the development of microscopes, and other technological advancements in film and photography.

The Hubble Space Telescope is an extremely complex piece of equipment. Yet, at its heart lies a system of mirrors and lenses designed by optical engineers.

HOW LIGHT WORKS

Visible light is part of the **electromagnetic spectrum**—a range of types of energy that travel as waves through air, matter, and even space. The electromagnetic spectrum includes **X-rays**, **infrared**, **ultraviolet**, and **microwaves** as well as light.

COLORED LIGHTS

Light that appears white—such as sunlight or light from an uncolored bulb—is actually made up of different colors of light. Sir Isaac Newton demonstrated this in 1666. He used a **prism** of glass to split white light. The light separated in the prism, casting out a rainbow of different colors. We see a similar effect after a rainstorm. Sunlight is split by tiny droplets of rain in the air, creating a rainbow.

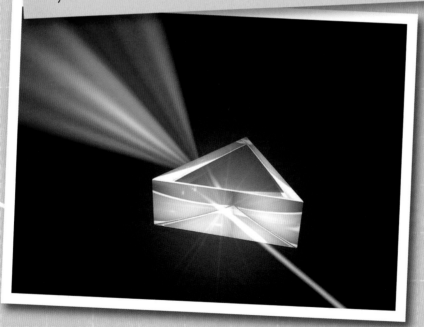

*As a beam of white light enters and then leaves a glass prism, light of different colors is **refracted** (bent) by different amounts and splits into the colors of the rainbow.*

Bundles of energy

A photon is a microscopic packet of energy. It is the basic unit of electromagnetic **radiation**, which forms invisible waves of energy, such as X-rays, infrared light, and sunlight.

Transparent materials: Optical engineers need to understand the light-carrying properties of materials. Light can travel through space or transparent materials. Light will not pass through a material if there is enough energy in the light's photons to disturb the **electrons** of the material.

If a photon does not have enough energy to disturb electrons, it passes through and the material is transparent. Glass is an example of such a material— photons of visible light don't have enough energy to move electrons in glass.

FIBER OPTICS

Light travels more quickly than anything else. That makes it useful in communications, because it can carry data over long distances very fast. Fiber optic cables are made of very thin glass or plastic fibers. They carry data as tiny pulses of light. Fiber optic cables were developed in the 1970s, and are essential to Internet and television services.

An engineer checks the high-quality glass that will be used to make optical fibers.

HOW ENGINEERS WORK WITH LIGHT

Light waves behave in the same way as other waves—even waves in water. Optical engineers use this information to change the direction and strength of light.

Tools of the trade: lenses and mirrors

Light rays pass through a lens, but bounce back from a mirror. Engineers use flat mirrors to redirect light without focusing or scattering it. They use curved mirrors or lenses to focus or scatter light.

LIGHT IS POWER

A solar power station collects energy from sunlight. Engineers calculate the angles at which a large number of mirrors must be placed to reflect all the sunlight that falls on the mirrors onto a single point. At this point (the focus of the collected mirrors), a **receiver** gathers the energy from the sunlight to store and convert it to electrical power.

A solar power plant reflects sunlight onto a central tower that collects the heat. It will be used to generate electricity.

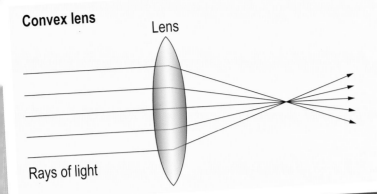

Convex lens

Lens

Rays of light

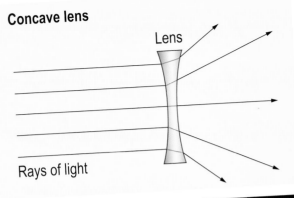

Concave lens

Lens

Rays of light

As light moves from one substance to another (e.g., air to glass), its direction of travel is changed. This is called refraction. Rays of light traveling through a flat window all change in the same way, so we don't notice a difference. But when rays of light fall on the surface of a curved lens at different angles, they are refracted differently (above). Engineers can use this to **magnify** an image.

A mirror reflects light. The light rays bounce back at the same angle as they strike the mirror. Engineers can use arrangements of flat or curved mirrors to send light in one direction, scatter it, or focus it on a single point.

Light rays passing through a convex lens come together to make objects appear larger. Concave lenses spread light apart to make smaller, more detailed images.

WORKING TOGETHER

Optical engineers often work closely with other types of engineers. An optical system fits into an instrument or casing made by mechanical engineers, and often works with an electronics system and computer components produced by software engineers. Optical engineers make calculations to figure out how light will move through a system from its source, such as a bulb, or a star.

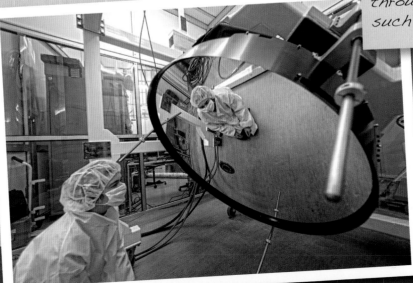

This mirror is only 0.08 inches (2 mm) thick. It will be used in a huge telescope to detect objects roughly four billion times fainter than those that can be seen with the eye.

LIGHT AND VISION

As light reflected from objects enters the eye, messages are sent to the brain to interpret what we are seeing.

How the eye works

The pupil of your eye is a hole, like the shutter of a camera. Behind it, a clear lens focuses incoming light rays so that they fall on the **retina**—the inside surface of the back of the eye. The retina has special light-detecting **cells**. When light falls onto a cell, a signal goes to the brain through the nerves. The brain creates an image from these signals.

Focusing light: The lens in your eye is a converging lens—it brings light rays together to focus them at a point (the **focal point**). If you have perfect vision, that point is on the retina. When the lens is the wrong shape, the focal point can be somewhere behind the back of the eye or somewhere in front of it.

People wear corrective lenses, or glasses, to move the focal point to the right place in the eye. Another option is to have surgery to reshape the retina so that the focal point falls on its surface. The distance from a lens to the focal point is called the **focal length** of the lens. Lenses with different thicknesses have different focal lengths. An optometrist chooses the best lenses to correct a person's vision.

Someone who is nearsighted has trouble seeing things at a distance.
Someone who is farsighted has trouble seeing things up close, such as reading a book.

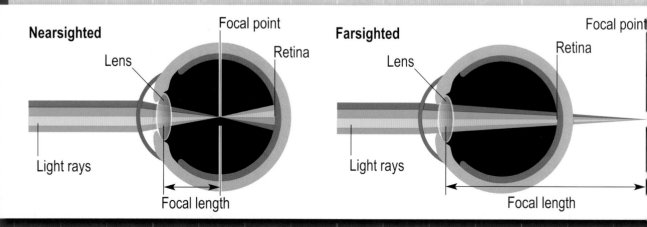

Nearsighted
Focal point
Retina
Lens
Light rays
Focal length

Farsighted
Focal point
Retina
Lens
Light rays
Focal length

PIONEER IN OPTICS

Ernst Abbe (1840-1905) has been called the father of modern optics. He worked in Germany, developing improvements to lenses and equipment that used lenses. He was the first person to find ways to measure and calculate how lenses work. Before his time, most work with optics was based on trial and error.

A contact lens sits on the surface of the eye. It improves vision by changing the angle of incoming light rays to make up for errors in the eye's lens.

ARTIFICIAL VISION

Optical engineers are working to develop artificial vision systems that can be used by computers and, eventually, by people who cannot see at all. The most exciting development is an artificial retina—a tiny arrangement of light **sensors** that can be implanted in the eye. When light strikes a sensor, it sends an electrical signal to the brain, just as the real retina does. The device is powered by the light that falls on it!

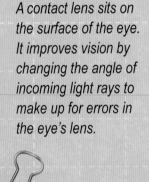

Optical engineers manufacture artificial retinas. Each contains a film of diamond, the only material with properties that are safe to use in the body.

HISTORY OF OPTICAL ENGINEERING

The first people to explore the properties of lenses and mirrors were Arab scientists working about 1,000 years ago.

First work in optics

The scientist Ibn al-Haytham, born in Basra (now in Iraq) in 965, was the first person to say that rays carry light and color to the eye. Working with **parabolic**, or curved, mirrors, he discovered how light is refracted off surfaces. Abu al-Biruni (973–1048) first discovered that light travels much faster than sound. In 1309, another Arab scientist al-Farisi explained how white light refracted through raindrops is split into separate colors, making a rainbow.

Ibn al-Haytham, one of the earliest scientists to work on the properties of light.

One of the first telescopes was made by Galileo in 1609. This painting shows Galileo demonstrating his device.

Using lenses: The first optical instruments to use lenses were spectacles, made in Italy in the 13th century to help nearsighted people.

Telescopes and microscopes appeared in Europe in the late 16th and early 17th centuries. A basic microscope has two magnifying lenses in a tube. The simplest telescopes used a similar arrangement, but reflecting telescopes, which use an array of mirrors, soon proved to be better. Sir Isaac Newton made the first successful reflecting telescope in 1668.

A WHOLE NEW WORLD

When the Belgian scientist Antonie van Leeuwenhoek made his first microscope in 1675, the world changed forever. His skill at shaping lenses enabled him to make a more powerful microscope than all earlier attempts. He discovered that living plants and animals are made up of tiny cells, and that every drop of water and grain of soil is teeming with life.

Antonie van Leeuwenhoek

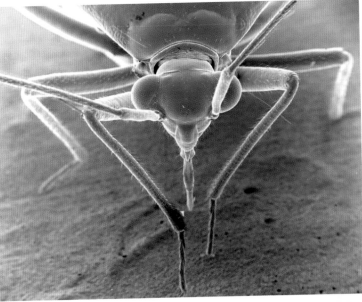

We can see what tiny bugs look like thanks to Antonie van Leeuwenhoek's invention of a powerful microscope.

Taking pictures

The first printed photographic image was made in France in 1822 by Joseph Niépce. A film camera focuses an image through a small hole (the shutter) onto a film coated with light-sensitive chemicals. Changing how long the shutter is open and the focal length of the lenses used affects how bright and sharp the image is when printed. The first digital camera was made in 1975. In a digital camera, light falls onto a light sensor in the camera instead of onto a film.

MORE USES FOR LIGHT

In the 20th century, optical engineering expanded into new areas, including data storage, telecommunications, solar power, and medical imaging.

Light and data

Alexander Graham Bell made the first attempt to transmit data—a telephone call—by light in 1880. It did not become practical until lasers and fiber optic technologies developed.

Lasers: A laser is an extremely focused beam of very high energy that can be used to cut through other materials. Lasers were developed at the same time by engineers in the United States and the U.S.S.R. (now Russia) in 1958. The light beam is created by using mirrors to bounce light of a single **wavelength** backward and forward, making it increasingly brighter. The light all leaves the laser traveling in the same direction. Lasers are used for cutting materials in industry and in surgery (especially on the eye), and are also components in many types of high-tech equipment. Optical engineers in many areas of science and industry need to understand and use lasers.

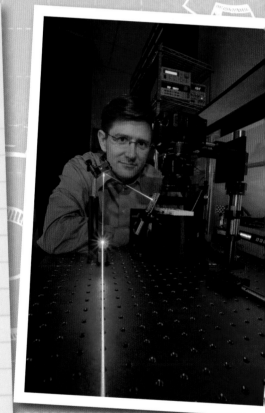

The beam from a laser is a single color, and spreads out very little.

AT HOME WITH LASERS

CDs became available in 1982. A CD is a molded plastic disc with a long spiral track starting in the center and made up of a series of bumps. The plastic is covered with a layer of aluminum that is coated with a protective layer of **acrylic**. The data is coded into the sequence of tiny bumps. When the disc is played, a laser follows the track in the plastic and is reflected off the aluminum layer. A sensor picks up the different reflections from the bumps and "flats," and sends the information for processing, turning it into music or other data.

A laser beam reads a CD. There is a laser inside every CD player and DVD player.

Medical imaging

Medical imaging involves taking pictures of the inside of the body. Sometimes this is done using visible light—when a tiny camera is fed down the throat to examine the stomach, for example. More often, it is done using techniques such as X-rays, **ultrasound**, or **magnetic resonance**. The image is built up by bombarding the body with rays of light and measuring how they are reflected or absorbed. People skilled in optics and medicine work together to design and build equipment like this and understand the data produced by the instruments.

A doctor uses medical imaging to examine a patient's blood vessels.

WORKING IN OPTICAL ENGINEERING

Optical engineers work in many different areas. There is great variety in the types of jobs available because optics can be used in so many ways.

Workplaces and jobs

Optical engineers might work in the high-tech industry, for makers of scientific instruments, in optometry, the military, health services, or the film and photographic industries. There is also work in **surveillance** and security, the police force, the media, and astronomy—and many other areas.

Skills needed

Optical engineers need a good knowledge of engineering and optics, excellent math, and skills in computing, electronics, and physics. They have to be good at teamwork, as they will have to work closely with engineers of different types. Good vision is often required.

Surveillance cameras are a common sight in many towns and cities.

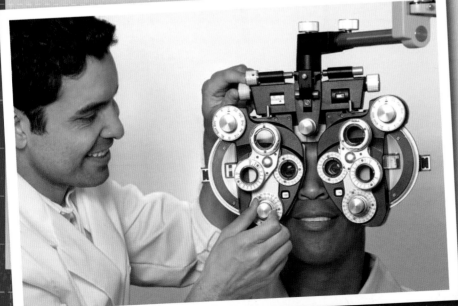

Optical engineers design the instruments optometrists use to test a patient's vision.

Optics software: Many optical engineers work with special software, which models the paths taken by light rays. This is called ray tracing. Ray-tracing software has many applications, from designing systems of lenses to adding the lighting effects to computer-generated animations.

Computer-generated animation uses complex ray-tracing software to create reflections and shadows as the virtual characters move.

PART OF THE BIGGER PICTURE

Optical engineers working for a German engineering company developed a new lighting system for the decks of ships. The system illuminates the deck evenly, leaving no dark patches. Each lamp uses an arrangement of special lenses to send light out in different directions. The lenses were first modeled on a computer by calculating the path and intensity (strength) of light falling on the lens surface and how the entire arrangement of lamps would interact over the whole deck.

A lighting engineer adjusts a studio light before a TV broadcast.

STARTING A PROJECT: PROBLEMS AND SOLUTIONS

At the start of every new project, optical engineers work with other engineers and designers to identify what is needed and come up with initial ideas.

Engineers use solar panels to capture the energy in sunlight.

Getting started: Often, the project begins with a need for a new product or solution. The aim might be to improve some existing technology or method. For example, one ongoing problem is that solar panels capture only a small amount of the energy in sunlight. Optical engineers are working to improve the methods used, to make the panels more **efficient**. At other times, the task is to find a completely new solution such as designing a camera to use in space. The first step is to draw up detailed specifications of the project. This describes what the product or technique will do.

Problems and possibilities: The project specifications also set out the criteria the project must meet and any constraints. The criteria are the goals the project must achieve. They are set by the customer. Constraints are limits. Some are practical, such as the properties of a material being used. For example a contact lens must be made of light, flexible materials that don't harm the eye. Some constraints are set by the customer, such as the cost and completion date (the deadline).

ONE CANDLE TO LIGHT THE OCEAN

People have built lighthouses for more than 2,000 years. A lighthouse uses lenses to amplify (strengthen) the light from one lamp and shine it out over the sea as a guide to ships. To make the light shine out brightly in all directions requires a large lens with a short focal length. But large lenses are very thick and heavy. Weaker lenses had to be used with the help of reflectors. Constraints on the size and weight of the lens made it difficult to build better lighthouses. The problem was solved in 1823 by Augustin-Jean Fresnel. He developed a lens, now called the Fresnel lens, with a stepped surface. It was much thinner and lighter than the convex lenses that were previously used in lighthouses. The Fresnel lens made lighthouses four times more effective. Fresnel lenses are still used in many lighting systems today.

A Fresnel lens (above) has lots of reflective surfaces to increase the power of light.

A lighthouse shines light far out over the sea as a warning to ships that they are near land.

IDEAS FACTORY

When it's clear what is needed, the next stage is to come up with suggestions of how to carry out the project.

Brainstorming: Brainstorming is a way of generating ideas. An engineer can brainstorm alone, but it's often most productive if several people are involved. Everyone makes suggestions, without worrying about whether they are good ideas or even if they are possible. The ideas are then evaluated at the end of the brainstorming session.

A NEW FORMAT FOR VIDEO

When it became possible to make digital videos, it was important to store video in files that lots of different types of equipment could understand. Fourteen different organizations were asked to suggest solutions which were then evaluated and compared. The best suggestion was developed into the MPEG format used today.

Feedback from early tablet users showed that they wanted a camera. Optical engineers figured out how to add to later models a camera that could record video.

Evaluating ideas: When different options have been suggested, engineers choose one or more of the ideas to develop further. They make a choice by deciding how well each idea meets the criteria for the project, and how well it deals with the constraints. They might also consider how long it will take to carry out, how much it will cost, the likelihood that it will be successful, and any risks involved—such as using untried techniques or new materials. They develop computer models to test the more promising solutions.

TOWARD HOLOGRAPHY

Sometimes, constraints that make a project impossible are later overcome. The Hungarian scientist Dennis Gabor worked on electron microscopes, which use beams of electrons to create an image of very small samples. In 1947, he realized that he could use the same techniques to create holographs—three-dimensional images. But he could not develop the project further because there was no way to target the beams of light with great accuracy. Only when laser technology was invented did holographs become possible. Two American engineers used Gabor's technique with a laser and created the first holograph in 1962.

A holographic image looks three dimensional, but is made entirely of light.

FIRST ATTEMPTS

When different options have been suggested and considered, engineers choose the best idea and develop it further.

*Modeling and prototypes: Projects in optical engineering often involve very expensive processes. Before making anything, engineers build a **prototype**—a small-scale, working version that can be tested and evaluated. Often, stages or components can be prototyped and tested separately. To save money and resources, engineers often use computer modeling to test new designs before producing the physical object. When the design performs well in software tests, a physical prototype is made.*

Ray tracing

Optical engineers use ray-tracing software to see how lenses or other components will behave. It shows the path of rays of light, how they fall onto objects, and how they are reflected or refracted. An engineer can adjust a design by changing the settings—such as lens size, position, focal length, material—and see immediately how the new settings perform. Nothing has been manufactured, so mistakes and extra trials cost very little.

An engineer tests the prototype of an unmanned aerial vehicle (UAV). The UAV has an optical guidance system based on how a fly's vision works!

SPACE TESTS

Lenses that will be used in space are first tested in air and, when they work well there, are tested in a **vacuum**—conditions that mimic space. Testing in a vacuum costs more than testing in air, but testing in space costs even more!

A LOOK INSIDE

Surgeons performing laparoscopic (keyhole) surgery work through a small hole in the body. They use tiny cameras to look inside and see the area they are working on, such as part of the stomach or heart, but they can only see a very restricted view. In 2012, an optical engineering team at the University of Arizona worked with surgeons to design a new laparoscopic camera. The main requirement was that it could provide both a wide-angle view and a **high-resolution** image at the same time, allowing surgeons to see a small area in detail. The camera now works, but the team needs to work on how best to display the images to the surgeon.

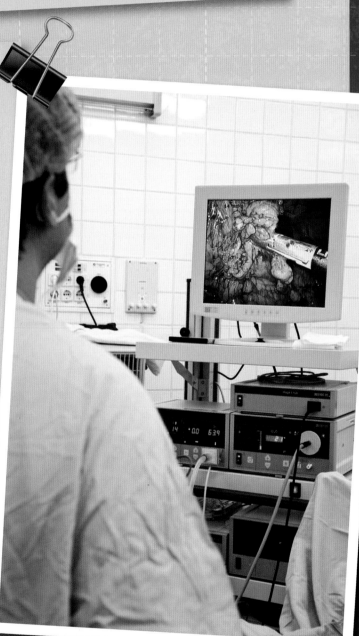

A surgeon watches a monitor while carrying out a surgical procedure. A camera inside the patient shows him what is happening.

REFINING THE PROJECT

Testing and evaluating a prototype often reveals limitations in a design. Maybe it doesn't work quite as expected, or the materials turn out to be unsuitable. For instance, a lens used outdoors might **distort** in the heat of the Sun so some protection or a different material is needed. Sometimes, improvements or other possibilities become clear during testing.

Understanding the results:
Testing a prototype can reveal problems that were not anticipated. Engineers then have to return to the design process, fitting new requirements and limitations into the design stage, refining the solution, and making and evaluating new prototypes. When the prototype behaves satisfactorily, the product can be manufactured and delivered.

Unexpected feedback

Occasionally, feedback comes later, when a product has been in use for a while. Soft contact lenses used to be completely clear, but many are now made with a slight blue tint. This does not make any difference to their optical performance, but makes it easier for them to be found when they are dropped!

A scientist runs some tests on a set of double-sided solar cells.

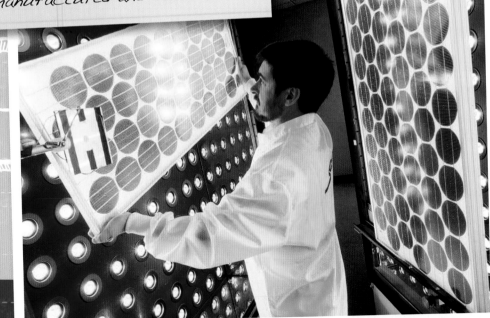

Optical engineers are helping astronomers to find exoplanets—planets similar to Earth—orbiting other stars.

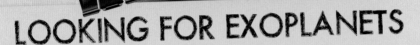

LOOKING FOR EXOPLANETS

NASA's search for exoplanets—planets in other solar systems—presents challenging problems for optical engineers. The brightness of a distant star makes it impossible to see planets near it. NASA engineers developed coronagraphs—special arrays of mirrors that concentrate the glare from the star's light into one spot and cut down distortion. They should work to clear the view for spotting planets. But there are always tiny errors, called aberrations, in any telescope's optics. The coronagraph did not work well enough to reveal Earth-sized exoplanets.

Engineers needed a new solution to enable the coronagraph to do its work. They built an array of small mirrors, each of which can actively change shape as necessary. These make up for the errors so that the coronagraph accurately removes the glare and exoplanets are visible.

This optical device is used in NASA's new system for looking for exoplanets.

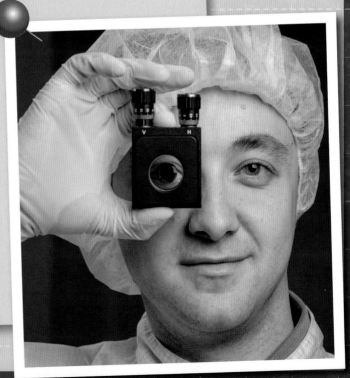

DESIGN CHALLENGE: MAKE A PERISCOPE

The best way to understand the design process and how it works is to try it yourself.

1: The problem: Your task is to make a simple optical device—a periscope. A periscope contains a set of mirrors and is used in submarines to look at what is happening on the surface of the water. You can use a periscope to see around corners or over walls.

2: Requirements and constraints: Think about how you want to use your periscope. This will help you to make decisions about its design. How long should it be? You can see over a tall wall if you have a long periscope, but it will need to be made of a rigid material so that it doesn't flop over. If you want to use it in water, it will need to be waterproof.

3: Brainstorm!: What types of material are available to you? Look online for ideas and designs. Compare them with what is possible for you and what you want to do with your periscope. Sketch your ideas.

The periscope of a submarine sticks up above the waves so that those on board can see what is happening at the surface.

4: Choose a solution: Compare the designs and ideas you have. Which best suits your requirements and what you have available? Are there any you have to rule out for some reason?

5: Make a prototype: Make a periscope using the materials and design you have chosen. It must be fully working, but is not your final version. For example, you don't need to fix the mirrors in place firmly. Fix them so that you can adjust them if they are not quite right. You don't need to decorate or color the outside.

6: Test your prototype: Try out your periscope. Does it work? Is it rigid enough? Is it too heavy or a difficult shape to hold easily?

7: Improve the design: Can you make your periscope better? Perhaps you could use different materials. How you will fix the mirrors firmly so that they don't wobble? Test it again when you have made all your improvements.

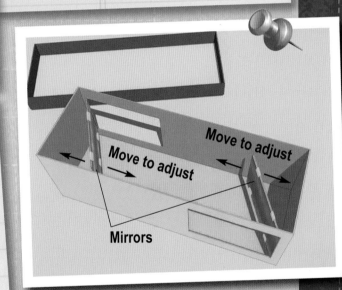

You could cut out two holes in the sides of an old shoebox and attach a pair of mirrors inside to make your periscope.

8: Communicate the design: Write up instructions for making your periscope, with diagrams. Make sure your instructions are clear, so that someone else could follow them. Add a diagram that shows the path of light rays going through your periscope so that it's clear how it works.

INTO THE FUTURE

At the cutting edge of optical engineering, engineers and scientists work closely together. Light and other forms of electromagnetic radiation that behave in the same way are used in increasingly varied ways.

Laser tools

Laser beams have many uses in engineering and science. Laser tools do the same job as normal tools without having to make physical contact with materials. Laser tweezers are used to nudge and move very tiny particles such as single cells or even single **molecules**. Laser tape measures can calculate long or short distances. The laser is bounced off a surface and calculations based on the reflection indicate the distance. They can be used in very restricted, inaccessible, or dangerous spaces. The ways in which laser tools can be used are constantly growing.

Measuring with a laser gauge gives a more accurate result than using a tape measure.

Seeing straight

The shape of the eye is important to how well we can see. Optometrists have always corrected vision by providing an extra lens to move the focal point within the eye. They have recently started to use a new technique, called orthokeratology, which uses **compression** contact lenses to reshape the eye. The lenses are worn during the night while a person sleeps. The success of the technique requires precise understanding of the shape of the eye and how it needs to be changed to refocus light through the lens.

SAIL AWAY

One of the most exciting developments for the future is the solar sail—a proposed way of moving spacecraft in space. As light falls on the sail, it pushes the craft through space!

Nanotechnology is being used to produce tiny solar cells, which could improve the way we capture energy from the Sun.

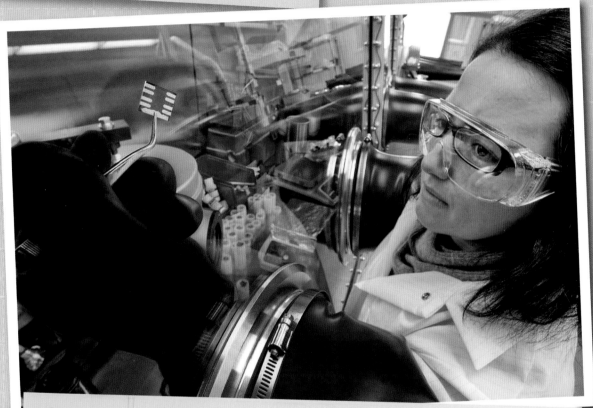

The power of light: Finding new ways to gather solar power on a small scale is a growing field as people become more concerned about using environmentally-friendly energy. Some new developments use **nanotechnology**—technology so small it can be seen only with a microscope—to make new light-sensitive materials that are lightweight, flexible, or transparent. One idea is a tent that can collect sunlight to power equipment inside it!

LEARNING MORE

BOOKS

Colleen Kessler, *A Project Guide to Light and Optics*, Mitchell Lane, 2011

Nicolas Brasch, *Tricks of Sound and Light*, Smart Apple Media, 2011

Leon Gray, *Light*, Gareth Stevens Publishing, 2013

Anna Claybourne, *Glaring Light and Other Eye-burning Rays*, Franklin Watts, 2013

Sally Hewitt, *Light (Project Science)*, Franklin Watts, 2013

Michael Anderson, *Light (Introduction to Physics)*, Rosen Education Services, 2012

Chris Woodford, *Light: Investigating Visible and Invisible Electromagnetic Radiation*, Rosen Central, 2012

ONLINE

http://jwst.gsfc.nasa.gov
Find out about the latest space telescope that NASA is building, and how it works.

www.physics4kids.com/files/light_intro.html
Find out all about light and how it works.

PLACES TO VISIT

There are many large telescope centers you can visit, including:

The Very Large Array telescope at the National Radio Astronomy Observatory, New Mexico:
http://www.nrao.edu/index.php/learn/vlavc

Mount Wilson Observatory, near Pasadena, California:
http://www.mtwilson.edu/vis.php

Helen Sawyer Hogg Observatory at the Canada Science and Technology Museum, near Ottawa:
http://www.sciencetech.technomuses.ca/english/whatson/hogg_observatory.cfm

Gustav Bakos Observatory, Ontario:
http://astro.uwaterloo.ca/observatory/

GLOSSARY

acrylic Clear plastic that is stronger and lighter than glass

cells Microscopic units of living matter found in plants and animals

compression Squashing together

distort Twist or deform

efficient Work well, with no wasted effort

electromagnetic spectrum Range of forms of energy that exist as waves, including light, radio, and X-rays

electrons Small particles present in all atoms

focal length The distance between a lens and the point where light rays passing through the lens come together (focus)

focal point The point at which light rays passing through a lens come together (focus)

focus To bring light rays together at a single point

high-resolution With a great deal of detail

infrared An energy just outside the spectrum of visible light, which is given out by heated objects

lasers Very narrow, closely focused beams of light

magnetic resonance A process that uses low-energy radio waves to produce pictures of the body behind bone

magnify To make an image larger, or make something appear larger

microwaves Radio waves with a shorter wavelength, used in the cooking of food

molecules The smallest components of matter, made of one or more atoms

nanotechnology Technology that works with extremely small (microscopic) components

optometry The science of using optical instruments (especially lenses) to correct faulty vision

parabolic Having the form of a parabola— a shape like a U with slanting uprights (or V with a curved base)

prism A block of glass or other transparent material with flat sides, used to refract light

prototype Early version or model of a new object or process

radiation A process by which energy moves through a vacuum or through matter, when the matter is not necessary for the movement of energy

receiver Part of a solar power station at which sunlight is focused to collect energy

refracted To have changed the direction of light as it passed from one substance to another (e.g., from air to water)

retina The surface of the inside of the eye

sensors Devices for detecting energy in the form of light, heat, or sound

solar power Energy from the Sun

surveillance The process of watching a place or person for security purposes

telecommunications Communication methods that work over long distances using electromagnetic radiation, such as radio, TV, and phone

ultrasound Sound waves with a frequency higher than those humans can hear

ultraviolet Energy just outside the spectrum of visible light, with a shorter wavelength than violet light

vacuum Space in which no matter is present, not even air or another gas

wavelength The distance between wave peaks in any type of wave, including tidal waves, sound waves, and different types of electromagnetic energy

X-rays An electromagnetic wave with a very short wavelength, which can pass through many materials that visible light cannot

INDEX